NOV   2013

AN
AMISH
GARDEN

AN AMISH GARDEN

A Year in the Life of an Amish Garden

Laura Anne Lapp

Photography by Jeremy Hess

Good Books

Intercourse, PA 17534
800/762-7171
www.GoodBooks.com

All photography by Jeremy Hess

Design by Cliff Snyder

AN AMISH GARDEN
Copyright © 2013 by Good Books, Intercourse, PA 17534
International Standard Book Number: 978-1-56148-792-9
Library of Congress Control Number: 2013932402

Publisher's Cataloging-in-Publication Data
Lapp, Laura Anne.
  An Amish garden : a year in the life of an Amish garden / by Laura Anne
Lapp ; photography by Jeremy Hess.
  p. cm.
  ISBN 978-1-56148-792-9

1. Gardening --American. 2. Seasons --United States. 3. Amish --Social
life and customs. 4. Amish --Social life and customs --Pictorial works.
5. Amish --Pennsylvania --Lancaster County --Social life and customs
--Pictorial works. I. Hess, Jeremy. II. Title.

SB451.3 .L37 2013
712/.6/0973 --dc23   2013932402

CONTENTS

Acknowledgments

Thank you, my five "sister gardeners," for making this project possible. Without your gardens and input, this book would have been very slight.

Thank you, my three boys—Aiden (age five), Thomas (age three), and Micah (age two)—for keeping my life interesting and being my big helpers.

Last, and most important, thank you, John, for your help, support, and patience. You've helped me more than you know.

—*Laura Anne Lapp*

A Word from the Publisher

In order to respect the caution which members of the Amish church have about being photographed, we have not included frontal, face-on photos of adults in this book. No photo was included in this book without the author's approval, in respect for her religious convictions.

ABOUT AN AMISH GARDEN

This is my year-long diary of living with a garden. I didn't write a how-to manual. Instead, I've recorded the love, the uncertainty, the hard work of growing our family's vegetables, and also the immeasurable satisfaction of preserving our food when the garden is in full swing.

I asked five other gardeners, friends and family members whose gardens and gardening skills I admire, if I could feature their gardens, along with mine, in *An Amish Garden*. We all garden differently, and I wanted to give a fuller picture of life with a garden than just my own.

"Barbie Mom" is my dear mother-in-law who lives just across the field from us and who has given me more

gardening advice than anyone else. She is a true gardener who loves everything about her garden.

Esther is a friend and practically my next door neighbor. She's older than I am and a very experienced gardener. Her gardens are the perfect ones—with straight, straight rows and no weeds. I strive to be like Esther.

Salome, my sister-in-law, lives down the road on the Lapp family home farm with her husband and six children. Salome has a gigantic garden and preserves a huge amount of food for her growing family. I always feel like I'm play gardening next to her.

Winey (her nickname since childhood; her real name is Anna) is my younger sister. She lives with her husband and three boys on a small farmette where they raise minia-ture horses. Winey's garden is much like Esther's. I don't think I've ever seen a weed there. Winey is very creative and loves to add interesting touches to her garden and flower beds.

Last, but definitely not least, is Becky, my other younger sister. She lives in a little ranch house with her husband and three children. Becky is the one who inspires me to start plants by seed. She does that every year and makes it look so tempting. Becky is also known for never throwing out any plants that have sprouted.

Welcome to our gardens!

— Laura Anne Lapp

JANUARY

This has been a very unusual January so far. It's the middle of the month, and we still haven't had any snow or ice to speak of. I have little creeping weeds all over my flower beds.

My neighbor Esther tells me that if I had a hot bed I could be planting now. I think that would be lovely. Imagine eating fresh radishes and spring onions in January! Sure, you can buy both onions and radishes year-round, but they never taste as good as fresh out of the garden.

When the weather is like this I get really impatient for spring. Everyone knows winter isn't over yet, but it's frustrating when I know it's too early to do anything outside, but it feels almost warm. I'm sure that when I send for my seeds and start planning the garden, the next few months will go fast.

Will six Roma tomato plants—the plum type that work best for sauces—be way too many? I'm starting my seed order, and I'm trying to remember how many Roma plants I had last year. I think it was only two, and this year I want many more.

Since I've discovered my new pizza sauce recipe, I know I'll need to can lots more than I did last year. The sauce is so delicious and so simple—it's only tomatoes, salt, pepper, garlic, and oregano. It tastes exactly like a tomato fresh out of the garden. I declare you can almost taste the sunshine.

My husband John designed and built our house. While the house was built for us, an Amish family, John designed it so that it could also function as a house for an "English" family. The patio doors on the side piece of the house are wide enough that they could be replaced by a garage door, turning that space into a garage.

PIZZA SAUCE

9 lbs. plum tomatoes, enough to make 13 cups fresh tomato puree

½ cup lemon juice, fresh *or* bottled

2 tsp. dried oregano

1 tsp. ground black pepper

1 tsp. salt

1 tsp. garlic powder

1. Quarter tomatoes and cook slightly so they're easier to puree. Add a small amount of water so the tomatoes don't scorch. Bring to a boil and boil for 3-5 minutes, just until the tomatoes are slightly soft. Pass through a Victorio strainer or food mill immediately.

2. Ladle puree into a large saucepan and add remaining ingredients. I always add more salt, pepper, oregano, and garlic salt than the recipe calls for. Boil hard for 15-30 minutes, until mixture is the consistency of a thin sauce.

3. Pour sauce into prepared jars, add lids, and process for 35 minutes.

Ever since John and I have been married, I've made homemade pizza for Saturday night supper. John's mother always did that when her boys were all at home, and I've adopted it as my own tradition. It's the one meal that we consistently enjoy, and it's one I feel good about serving. It's healthy, homemade, and easy. I also use lots of ingredients from my cellar. A jar of pizza sauce, one of applesauce, and another of pickles.

John taught the boys to cut up each slice of pizza into bite-size chunks and then dip the pieces into applesauce just before they eat them. When Aiden first started asking for that, I thought it was horrible, but now I just smile when the boys want applesauce on their plates. They all want a huge serving right beside their pizza for dipping ease. Every week we, or actually *they,* eat almost a quart of applesauce with their pizza. I'm thinking maybe an orchard would be a good idea for us.

SO MUCH TO DECIDE

I spent the morning paging through the seed catalogs, and I have a million ideas leaping through my mind. I love the idea of a privacy screen windbreak at the edge of the garden. There are many different plants to use for that, but I was reading about a hybrid willow tree. Of course, according to the catalog, nothing grows as well as they do. These trees thrive in poor soil, grow extremely fast, and do every other good thing they can think of to say about them. I tend to fall for those ads and always end up trying the product. Over the years I've won some and lost some.

In January everything sounds so good. I'm always ready to go outside again, and I have all these plans and dreams for the coming year. This time I'm determined to be a little more organized with my buying. I will write down exactly what I'm going to buy and where I plan to plant each vegetable. That way I shouldn't run out of space like I do every year.

I always try to remember how the vegetables held out the year before. Did I have enough or too many of each one? Of course I can't keep track of all of them, so I do a lot of guessing. I always tend to order more than I need, but that's not a big deal because I can always use those seeds later in the year, or even save them for the next year.

I don't really know how much space each type of veggie takes, so that's another guess. I'm sure there are gardeners who never have extra seeds or rows that are too long with no seeds to go into them. But I've never been too technical when it comes to my garden, and I probably never will be. I enjoy gardening my way!

I think I'll try pole beans. I know they won't take up a lot of space, and I think their height would be quite attractive in a vegetable garden. I keep reminding myself to save space for a lot more Roma tomatoes. No more relying on bought pizza sauce, which now tastes terrible compared to our own homemade.

December and January are a grateful rest period for the gardener. This morning I'm really glad to stay inside, sip my coffee, and watch the world grow gradually whiter with a dusting of flurries. The snow is beautiful, turning everything into oblique shapes. The grasses bow their heads, touching their snowy plumes to the ground. The raised beds' sharp edges slowly turn into fluffy white pillows. It's hard to imagine now, the beds overflowing with brilliant zinnias and blooming sunflowers. All that color has disappeared and turned into a white wonderland. Such a contrast, and so much beauty in each season.

I would love to add a whole new part to the garden this spring, but I'm not sure we can manage it this year. John and I have been considering adding a new walled or boxed-in part with a grape arbor and perhaps a few fruit trees.

Running through the middle of the garden, I'd

like to plant a whole row of butterfly bushes, with other plants mixed in that butterflies love—bee balm maybe, or lantana. Then I'd like to make a little terrace and put our patio bistro set down there. *Voila!* I'd have a butterfly viewing station. That's my Dream Number One for this spring.

Surprise! I am sure seed catalogs come earlier every year. Last week three arrived in my mailbox on the same day. I couldn't believe it. Is there anything as lovely as leafing through a seed catalog in the dead of winter? Just reading the descriptions of various plants makes the sun come out and breezes start blowing. I can spend hours poring over the pages and dreaming for the coming year.

Sometimes I send for the seeds, and other times I just get ideas from the catalogs and buy the seeds at local greenhouses. I think I'll send for them this time. I was a little disappointed last year in the lack of choice at the greenhouse.

Salome lives on the original Lapp family farm where my husband grew up. Along with a large organic garden, she and her husband, Elvin, also run an organic dairy and grow and bale their own hay.

I clipped the heads off last summer's sunflowers and dried them in the barn. In the winter, I pushed the heads into the bird feeder, stuck the dried stems into the ground around the feeder, and even tied a few heads to the trees. The woodpeckers and nuthatches, the birds that really like to dig for their food, peck the seeds from the sunflower heads.

WEATHER— AN ENDLESS GUESSING GAME

What will the weather be like this year? Last year's gardening season was quite discouraging. It was so very rainy and cool in the spring that it seemed like forever until I could finally plant the garden. After it dried off a little and everything was doing well, we got hot, dry weather that completely toasted the garden.

The answer for that is watering, of course, but for some reason that's my least favorite part of gardening. I'm just annoyed by having to pull hoses around, connecting and disconnecting them, then turning the water on and off, fastening the sprinkler and finally giving everything a thorough soaking. It sounds silly, but it just takes a lot of patience. John bought me a watering wand last summer, and that really helped.

Late last summer, the hot weather finally moved on and things became very rainy again. In fact, we had another round of monsoon weather. I remember there was a short period of dry weather near the end of August when the potatoes could've been harvested. But we were busy with other things, and then it started to rain again and we couldn't dig them for weeks. The plants actually started growing again, and the potatoes were not the greatest.

But now, looking back over the whole year, things weren't so bad. And it's a lovely feeling to go to the basement for canned goods or to grab a bag of corn from the freezer, knowing there are no additives or artificial anything in the food I processed myself.

I don't want to be ungrateful, and I thank God for the many blessings he bestows on my family and me every day of the year. As any gardener knows, dealing with Mother Nature's whims is just one of the many joys and challenges of the job.

WHY GARDEN ANYWAY?

All Amish children grow up with gardening as a regular chore and way of life. As a mom, I hope I can teach my boys to enjoy and appreciate a garden for what it is. For the practical gardener, it means the freshest vegetable and fruit supply to be had. It is nature's bounty at its finest, just waiting to find its way into canning jars as pickles, sauces, jams, and jellies.

For the hobby gardener, it is the beauty of the garden and the satisfaction of having planted the perfect combination, whether flowers, herbs, or vegetables. I would class myself a mixture between hobby and practical.

I love gardening best for its beauty—the beauty of planting a tiny seed or sprout and watching it turn into a full-grown plant. Flowers are my favorite, but I'm learning that vegetables have a beauty all their own. It's hard to find a blossom anywhere that's more amazing than a zucchini plant in full bloom. The plants have large, dark green leaves that are rather prickly to the touch. Nestled under those leaves are breathtakingly delicate blooms of pale orange. I'm always amazed that something so plain as a zucchini emerges from all that beauty!

On the other hand, flowers don't need to produce anything practical to earn their keep. It's for beauty alone that we plant them. On a cold January day, it's balm to this gardener's soul to look back and remember the rows of brilliant zinnias waving in the warm sunshine. I reassure myself that in three or four months it will be time to head outside again.

Winey's canning shelves are stocked with the relish, peppers, spaghetti sauce, and salsa that she canned last summer.

HOW AND WHEN TO PLANT?

I'm trying to figure out if I should start any plants by seed this year. There are so many pros and so few cons, that I'm not sure why I wouldn't. I love the fact that I can try anything without wasting much money, because most seeds are relatively cheap.

I saw a little gadget in the one catalog that helps you make paper pots out of old newspaper. You fashion the little flowerpots, fill them with soil, and simply sprinkle the seeds on top. Supposedly the seeds survive until it's time to plant them outside in the garden. Then you just dig a hole and plop the whole thing in. The newspaper disintegrates and mixes into the soil.

It sounds like a great idea, but last year I used peat pots and I wasn't very impressed. The process is the same, except the pots are made of peat, a type of moss-like material that also disintegrates.

The only problem with the peat pots was that they were very hard to water correctly. Too little water isn't good for obvious reasons, and too

much is bad, too. I found that the water didn't drain well, so the pots got really yucky before it was time to plant them outside. In the future, I think I'll simply start my tomatoes in three- or four-inch terra cotta pots. They're relatively cheap, and I can reuse them. That will save me the hassle of trying to make little newspaper pots.

That brings me to my second problem with starting seeds inside. When exactly should I plant them inside? I think I usually plant the seeds too early, and then the plants get long and "leggy" and seem very fragile when it's time to plant them outside.

The method that works best for me, at least for flowers, is to fill a shallow bowl with potting soil or with seed starting mix—about five or six inches deep—and then sprinkle a whole packet of seeds on top. I lightly cover the seeds with a thin layer of potting soil. I put the bowls in a sunny window and wait until they sprout.

After they're tall enough—anywhere from

three to four inches high—I just pull them up by clumps and transplant them into the garden. This works well for little seedlings like marigolds, most herbs, and all kinds of flowers. Of course, for vegetables or anything for which you work with individual plants, that wouldn't work. And some seeds just do better when they're sown directly into the soil. Of course, I wait until there's no more chance of frost.

I've learned my lesson with zinnias. Every year I plant them along the edge of the garden. They're my favorite summer flower, simply because they're so hardy. I used to start them inside in early spring, but I've discovered they do better sown directly into the garden soil. I plant packet after packet of seeds, so I have a thick row of zinnias. It's hard to find a braver, more cheerful flower than a zinnia. When the weather is unbearably hot and most other garden plants are wilting, the zinnia is in its glory.

Sunflowers also do better sown directly into the garden because the seedlings are so fragile. That seems strange, because sunflowers are actually quite sturdy, once full-grown.

I've found that vine crops like cucumbers, watermelon, and cantaloupe are all pretty easy to start, whether you put the seeds outside straight into the soil, or inside in pots, or even buy young plants at the greenhouse. I've tried all three ways, and I really don't think it makes much difference which you choose.

FEBRUARY

GARDENING PERKS

It's the first of February already. Time has begun moving so fast this winter that, before I know it, I'll be digging in the dirt.

I just read an article in a magazine about the health benefits that come from dirt and soil while you work in the garden or dig in your flowerbeds—or whenever your hands are in contact with dirt. Supposedly your body absorbs minerals that are in the soil, and those minerals are thought to be a natural anti-depressant. They boost the body's ability to make "feel good" thoughts or feelings or whatever you call them. Now I know why I'm happier and more content in the summertime. It's the dirt!

THE SEED ORDER

This morning I put my seed order into the mailbox. This year I'm right on schedule with the order. Often I wait until too late, and then I'm left scrambling at the last minute, trying to get all the seeds together and ready to plant. I sent for tomatoes, peppers, carrots, pole beans, red beets, radishes, lettuce, and sweet corn, of course.

I didn't order onion sets or seed potatoes. I prefer to buy them from the local seed store. I guess you don't actually call them seed stores. The proper wording is probably "agricultural supply store." I always feel safer buying onions and potatoes when I can see them.

I don't know exactly what makes a bad onion set, but I choose the ones that are

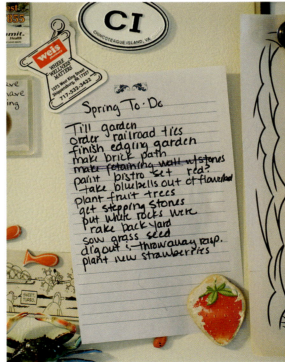

plump, not shriveled and sickly-looking. The same with seed potatoes—nice, plump, smooth potatoes with plenty of "eyes," the little protrusions where the plants start to sprout. I've already planted potatoes left over from the previous year's crop, but they definitely do not produce the best results. They just don't do as well as seed potatoes.

Sometimes I'm not sure if growing our own potatoes is worth the bother, but John's usually in charge of them. You've got to plant them and then hill them, mounding up the soil around them after they're tall enough. Then you have to mulch them to keep the weeds down. Last year we didn't mulch, and we discovered that mulch makes a huge difference. The whole

This is always the fun part—filling out the seed catalog order form. This year I added pole beans and pattypan squash to the usual list of seeds. Gardening is actually starting now!

garden just looks much neater after it's mulched. And it really cuts down on weeding. It's more work initially, but it sure makes it worthwhile later on in the season.

My trial plant this year is pole beans. I love raised beds, but sometimes they call for a little

creativity since they do limit the size of each patch. Green beans did well last year, but I had to plant about three raised beds-full to have enough plants, and that didn't leave a lot of space for other things. So I decided I'll try vertical this year. I think they'll look pretty, too.

Hopefully I, or John, will be able to make a trellis like I saw in a magazine. It looks kind of like a teepee made out of bamboo poles, all fastened together at the top. I'm almost sure they were tied only with string, but, knowing my husband, he'll come up with something very efficient and durable.

I'm planning to have two trellises in one raised bed, or if that doesn't work, one trellis per bed with carrots planted in the rest of the space. That would probably be prettiest. I really shouldn't worry so much about the visual side of gardening, but that's the part I really love.

Don't get me wrong. I love the fresh food and the work that goes into the garden. But sometimes the work gets overwhelming and tiring. That's when you need the beauty of the garden to keep you inspired.

I normally pick one seed catalog and buy most of my seeds from that company. Last year Winey and I ordered from one company, and Becky ordered from a different one. Becky thought her plants were nicer!

Becky finds it works best if she waters her little peat pots of tomatoes by dipping them in a bowl.
She lets the seedlings drip dry in the bowl for a little bit before returning them to the tray.

STARTING THE TOMATOES

Yesterday my sisters and I were discussing our gardens and whether or not we'll start seeds indoors this spring. I never tried tomatoes because I was always afraid they wouldn't do well, but Winey said she did it last year and had a wonderful tomato crop.

Becky agreed and said you can't beat starting your own, partly because it's so cheap you can try as many varieties as you want to. So I decided to follow suit and promptly ordered tomato seeds. I sent for Roma tomatoes, of course, plus yellow ones for eating raw, and also cherry tomatoes. I think that maybe if the boys see these tiny little tomatoes and are allowed to pick them, they'll sample them and learn to enjoy them.

I'm going to start the seeds in small pots, maybe three-inch ones, and very carefully put three or four seeds into each pot. After they're sprouted and I have

too many little seedlings, I'll snip some off and let the others prosper.

I read somewhere that you should never pull out a seedling if you have too many in one pot, because it can disturb the roots of the remaining plants. So I cut off the weaker ones, the ones that look frail and not as sturdy, and then the stronger ones can thrive.

I remember when I was a little girl, Grandma Kauffman would save seeds from the tomatoes that she raised in her garden and start new plants that way. She would ever so carefully pick the seeds out and lay them on a paper towel to dry. I don't know how long she dried them or where she stored them over winter, but she always had rows of paper cups on her windowsills in the spring, bursting with tiny little flowers and vegetables plants.

CLEANUP AND STRAWBERRIES

Yesterday was unseasonably warm for February, so the boys and I went for a walk. They played on the swings while I wandered around in the garden. Why does a garden seem so much bigger in the wintertime? I know the dimensions are exactly the same, and the number of raised beds hasn't changed, but something makes it seems larger. Maybe it's because everything's so dead and brown. Last season I left the marigolds in the ground to see if they might reseed themselves and come back up. I doubt that they will.

I'm going to have quite the spring cleanup this year. I guess I was really sick of garden work by the end of the year, because there sure is a lot to do in it before I plant! Two of the raised beds are covered in grass clippings that are just completely matted and horrible. They have to be dug into the soil or covered with compost before I can plant.

I planted one raised bed with radishes in the fall. I remember we didn't eat them because they were very hot, so I left them in the bed as soil improvers. That bed will be pretty nice in the spring because everything has died back, and I'll work the radishes into the soil when I get ready to plant.

That brings me to my next problem. The strawberries are not doing well in the raised bed where I have them. I think they need more space. I asked Barbie Mom about it and she said strawberries do best if they're thinned out every year so the new shoots have space to grow. She's trying to make her raised strawberry bed work by pulling out the old plants and giving the "runners," or new plants, plenty of room. I think I'll just tear all the old plants out and start a new patch somewhere else.

My raspberries are not great either. They do okay, but I've never yet had a nice crop of berries, and honestly, I hate to pick them. The bushes are so ungainly and prickly, and Japanese beetles adore the berries. So all in all, they're hardly worth it. I have no patience for plants that need to be coddled.

So I think I'll get rid of the raspberries and start a new strawberry patch at the side of the garden where the raspberries have been. I can give the strawberries as much room as they need because, with the raspberries gone, that whole far side of the garden will be open. In fact, I'll probably add rhubarb beside the strawberries or in another raised bed. Rhubarb would be really attractive in a raised bed in the middle of the garden, because it's such a flourishing-looking plant.

I never draw a plan for the garden before I start planting. I try to remember what I had planted in each section the year before, so I can rotate the crops. Sometimes if I get stuck, John comes to the rescue. He's much more careful than I am and really thinks things through rather than guessing like I do.

OLD HAY MULCH

I have been having a mental argument with myself all week. Down in the woods, beyond the henhouse, there's a large pile of rotting hay. It's been there for about two years, and I know what I'm throwing away. Well, not throwing away exactly, but ignoring.

Old hay, or mulch hay—or hay that's been left outside in the weather for a while—is the very best mulch for a vegetable garden. It keeps the weeds down wonderfully and also keeps the soil moist for a long time. It's the greatest mulch for potatoes, especially, because after they're covered with a thick layer of mulch hay, you can virtually ignore them until it's time to dig them out in the fall.

Cucumbers are another crop that benefits greatly from a thick layer of old hay.

But that all seems rather insignificant when I think about pushing my wheelbarrow down to the edge of the woods, loading that smelly, slimy hay, and pushing it back up the slope toward the garden. Actually, the smell probably wouldn't be bad anymore. What really bothers me more than I like to admit are all the creepy crawlies that have lived in that pile the past couple of years.

Can you imagine the scores of spiders, bugs, and beetles that make their homes there? Not to mention the snakes and worms. Oh, and I'm sure there are snakes! I remember all too well, when I was a girl at home, Mom got a pile of old hay from the neighboring farmer, and we children had to help spread the awful stuff on the garden. More than one garter snake slithered out of that pile before we were done.

I know now since I'm a grown-up and have my own garden that there are definitely benefits to using old hay for mulch, but it's still difficult for me to face the creatures abiding there.

Maybe if I ask John very sweetly he'll do the hauling for me. Then perhaps I can, ever so gingerly, spread the hay around the vegetables with a long-handled fork and rake. I might even wear boots and gloves and then nothing can touch me. I know I would be so pleased to have my garden mulched with hay, because it really cuts down on weeding in the summer months. I'll just have to be strong and not mind the little creatures, and then it will all be fine.

My other option for mulch is buying mushroom soil, which works well, too. But it's expensive. I need yards and yards of it to cover the whole garden. I thought maybe I could do half and half this year, some hay and some mushroom soil. Mushroom soil makes the garden soil nice and soft and definitely helps with weeds.

Last year I didn't mulch at all, and I really missed it. Well, that's not true. I did use some grass clippings but they're not the best solution. They really mat together and create an almost solid barrier between the seeds or plants and the sun and rain. The rain could hardly soak through them. Grass clippings should go on the compost pile and decompose before they're used. They seem to work better like that. Although I did read somewhere that one man uses only grass clippings for his potatoes and loves it. So I may have to try that sometime.

MARCH

PLANTING

What a fun day we had! I finally planted the raised beds, and the boys were helping every step of the way. We've been talking about planting for weeks, so it was in the backs of their minds for a while.

The great thing about raised beds is that we don't have to wait for John to till the soil. We can just go ahead and plant whenever the boys and I are ready. When the day finally arrived, they were extremely excited and overly helpful!

We started by spreading granular fertilizer on each raised bed. Micah and Thomas got a little too enthused so we may have some very fertile corners.

Onions are easy for little boys to plant because the sets are bigger than seeds. I get the kids started with these, and then I plant the smaller seeds like radishes and beets.

Aiden was my big helper all day. He did a great job planting onions and beans, and then carefully covering his rows. We planted spring onions, radishes, red beets, and beans. For some odd reason I forgot to buy lettuce seeds, so I will have to get some. I cannot do without my "cream lettuce" in the spring!

In the evening when John came home, he tilled the main part of the garden. We usually call Dewalt to prepare our garden with a tractor, but this year John decided to rent a rototiller and do it himself. I loved doing it this way, because John is very cautious and does a great job with everything he tries.

So the garden looks absolutely wonderful. John went over the soil, back and forth a couple of times, and now it's so soft and crumbly. We think the mushroom mulch has made the soil so much better.

After John was done tilling, we planted potatoes. That's the one crop I don't plant by myself. I think planting potatoes is a man's job.

Making the rows is the hardest part, because they need to be really deep. So we always wait until John comes home to do the potatoes.

This year the little boys gladly sprinkled the fertilizer and Aiden helped plant. By seven-thirty that evening, we had three exhausted boys and a very happy mom. We had planted so many things in one day!

Becky claims it's too early to plant potatoes, but Barbie Mom has already planted hers. I decided to take Barbie Mom's advice about when to plant. She's been gardening much longer than I have, and I'm sure she knows what she's talking about. If my potatoes rot in the ground, Becky will have the last laugh.

The early spring vegetables are planted, but we'll have to wait to plant corn, beans, peppers, tomatoes, and other crops until the threat of frost is over. Barbie Mom's rule of thumb—and now mine, too—is to wait to plant them until Mother's Day. That's the easiest way to remember for me. Usually our area doesn't get frost after the middle of May.

The whole family adds the fertilizer to the soil before we place the potatoes.

WEEDS AND PREPARING THE SOIL

Every year I do the same thing. I don't keep after the weeds in the early spring, and they get a huge head start. That's the worst thing imaginable for a garden. It makes the job so much harder if you wait too long. If you can manage to get the weeds out when they're small, it's much easier and faster to keep a clean garden.

I must admit that flower beds come first in the spring. I love to clip and rake away all the winter's debris, and always, no matter how dead a plant looks, there's bound to be a tiny shoot pushing out of the soil. It's so reassuring every year. I never tire of that springtime miracle.

WEATHER AND PLANTING

I wonder if there's ever been a prettier March? People are planting garden and working outside the last few days. The temperatures have been in the upper sixties and low seventies all week. So gorgeous!

Esther planted some of her garden at the end of February, so she has lettuce and radishes sprouting. She also started some zucchini and cucumbers and covered them with plastic domes that look like miniature greenhouses. You can even twist their tops to vent them.

Trust Esther to have something like that. She's always ahead of the game when it comes to gardening. Always, she's the one who's serving fresh garden vegetables first in the spring. Lovely lady!

I wish I was as ambitious as she is. She always reassures me that I have three boys to care for, and hers are grown and gone. So maybe someday I'll be like her. Honestly, I doubt it though. I tend to be pretty laid back when it comes to gardening. I think I've learned that from John's mom. No huge rush in the spring, and she always has one of the nicest gardens around.

HERE WE GO!

Well, I've done my first day of outside work for this spring. Is there anywhere a lovelier feeling than stepping outside your front door, heading to the shed to load up your tools? My equipment is old-fashioned—a plain old hoe, a rake, and a hand-held trowel. Nothing beats those three tools. I love the purpose of having a particular job that needs to be done in the garden. Everything else in life goes on hold for a little while.

Today my agenda is to get rid of the raspberries and spread pulverized lime on the raised beds. It was a little chilly when I started, but I soon warmed up. What a job digging those prickly raspberries out! They're horrible. I have hundreds of tiny little thorns in my hands. Or it feels like that anyway. I dug up shovelfuls of roots and tried to pick them up by the soil covered parts, but somehow I still got piles of little thorns.

Today I drove Gina, our driving horse, up to Winey's and then we went to Becky's. At Becky's we unhitched the horse, tied her in the barn, and proceeded to pack up nine children in the wagon and stroller to walk to the neighboring farm. The Amish family that lives there raises sheep, and in the spring they have "open barn." The public can come tour the farm and get a chance to see all the baby lambs. The boys absolutely love it, and we usually go every year.

Lots of people were starting to get their gardens ready. Winey's garden was sprinkled with lime, and her husband was walking over to the neighbors to borrow a rototiller. Mose, Becky's

husband, was putting the finishing touches on two, new, raised beds. And on our walk to the farm we saw two different families preparing to rototill or spreading lime.

I noticed crocuses in bloom and daffodils getting ready to burst. How exciting it is every year to start anew!

I can't imagine living without the changing seasons. There's always a special loveliness when you're on the brink of a new season. Just today I was showing Aiden the tightly curled buds on the lilac bushes and explaining how warm sunshine causes them to open into leaves.

I'm always amazed by how fast things start to change when the weather warms up. Spring, I think, is the most amazing season with all the new beginnings. I'm always especially aware of God's awesome power and handiwork in the spring.

When Winey cleans out her miniature horses' stables, she puts the hay on a big pile and lets it compost before she spreads it on the garden. If she puts it on the garden straight from the stall, she finds that more weeds grow.

SEWING

Finally I'm finished with my sewing for this year. My goal every year is to be done with all sewing by the time I plant the garden. I made it this time. I absolutely hate to sit inside at my sewing machine when it's getting warm outside, and I could be getting the garden ready to plant or cleaning out the flower beds.

I think boys' clothing requires more sewing than girls'. Boys always have two pieces— shirts and pants. On the other hand, girls tend to be more picky with their clothes, while boys just grab whatever's on top of their pile, and that's what they wear that day. Pants are always the main project at this house. This year I made 13 pairs, and I'm trying not to notice that Aiden needs new pants for church.

Sewing is the only thing that I really don't enjoy about being a mom and housewife. If I weren't Amish, there's no way I'd ever sew! It is such a slow, sitting-down kind of job, and it always seems the more I try to hurry, the more I make mistakes. So slow and steady is my motto when I'm sewing.

Always at this time of the year, when it's getting warmer outside and the sun is shining so cheerfully, I have only one thing I want to do. Go outside! The boys have cabin fever, and I'm impatient with my sewing. It's simply time to get out!

APRIL

A GARDEN SURPRISE

This afternoon when I was taking the laundry off the line, I thought the garden seemed suspiciously green. I folded the laundry and put everything away, and then walked down to investigate.

I was completely shocked! I think every single radish seed that didn't sprout last fall was simply lying dormant, waiting for some rain and a bit of warm sunshine. My garden is absolutely green with tiny radish sprouts. It's horrible because these are tillage radishes, and they're overgrowing everything I've just planted. Their job is to rebuild the soil, not keep other plants from sprouting in the springtime. I can't even hoe or rototill the rows to keep the weeds down and encourage the other seeds to sprout. Looks like the radishes will just go on growing for now.

Later when the vegetables are tall enough, I'll run the rototiller through and mulch the radishes. But for now, I can only wait.

EARLY APRIL

I think this is the most annoying time of year for gardeners. My sisters and I were discussing it yesterday. The weather is beautiful, and we'd love to go work in the garden, but we really can't do much. The early vegetables I planted aren't tall enough to weed or rototill around them, so I have to wait.

It's too early to plant tomatoes, cucumbers, and zucchini, so again I have to wait. I don't like this limbo. Sure, there's always something to do outside, but right now it's an in-between time for everything.

The weather was so warm in mid-March that now in April it feels like it's much later than it is. So I'll just have to cool my heels and try to remind myself that in June and July, I'd be glad for a day when I didn't have much to do.

In my garden, the beds that are mulched have seeds growing in them. Most of the unmulched beds are waiting for tomato plants. One bed without mulch is planted with beans, but the plants aren't tall enough to mulch yet.

PEAS

This year I decided to try peas again. John and the boys aren't crazy about them, but I love them, especially fresh out of the garden. So I tilled a small strip of soil right beside the raised beds and planted three rows of peas. The boys didn't help because they were busy with a project of their own in the sandbox.

I made the rows as well as I could, which isn't ruler-straight. But I figured it would do for peas since we always put wire along the rows after the plants are about three or four inches high. Then the plants clamber up the wire, making it much easier to pick from them.

After the rows were made, I carefully dropped the seeds in one by one, then covered them with a thin layer of soil. Hopefully we'll get a good crop of peas this year and the boys will learn to enjoy them.

Confession time for the wasteful gardener. I was rototilling tillage radishes out of the newly planted pea patch the other day, when I lost all patience and started wildly whipping my rototiller from side to side, not caring what I plowed out. The peas were tiny little shoots that I could hardly discern from the radishes.

The entire time my mind was racing, and I was reassuring myself that it was fine to do this. At first I felt bad. Then I decided, "No, I won't be guilty. This is my garden, and if I don't think I can manage raising peas and processing them, there's no rule saying that just because I'm an Amish housewife, I have to raise peas!" Happiness settled on me after I decided that.

When I was a young girl at home, we always did row after row of peas. We'd get up early in the morning and stumble out to the garden without even pausing for breakfast. We would pick peas, complaining the whole time, groaning, and even arguing now and then. But we looked forward to settling onto the front porch with bowls in our laps to shell all the peas.

We always did them by hand, never taking them to the local Mennonite man who had a pea huller. Shelling peas was the one thing we enjoyed about raising them. We talked and laughed the whole time, our mouths moving as fast as our hands. It never seemed to take long to shell them.

Often, my dad's grandparents, who lived right across the road, would join us. It was one thing they could do that made them feel useful. Being teenagers at the time, we often grumbled when we saw them tottering across the road because

Winey dumps a bucket-full of pea pods into a stall for her miniature horses to eat.

we wanted to discuss things that were of interest to us and not listen to the "Old Dawdys," as we called them. Not many children get to grow up with grandparents and great-grandparents as their next-door neighbors.

When I remember how it was to help in the garden like that, I want my boys to have that same experience. But I must remind myself, that they're young yet. When they're 12, 10, and nine, we'll raise lots of peas, and they can help. This year we'll plant pumpkins where the peas were, and the boys will enjoy them much more.

They've all been talking about pumpkin pies, and Aiden informed me in strict tones that, "We have to plant pumpkins this year. We never had pumpkins in our garden."

I'm taking my five-year-old's advice. Pumpkins for peas sounds like a fair trade to me!

The solar panels on the side porch roof charge the 12-volt batteries that operate the lights in our house. In the wintertime we use gas lights in the kitchen because the days are shorter, and so the solar panels can't provide enough power to keep the batteries charged.

RADISHES

My tillage radish catastrophe seems to be getting worse and worse. Every time I go down to the garden, there are more. I suggested to John that maybe we could just throw our mushroom mulch on top of the radishes and hope it kills them. But he didn't seem to think that was a great idea. Of course it's not; it was just born of desperation.

Every evening I'm in the garden now, pulling out those hideous things! I still want to try them again this fall, though, because Barbie Mom's and Salome's turned out fine. Salome thinks they should be planted by mid- to late August so they're growing and dying off at the right times. Then they won't interfere with the other plants.

Barbie Mom said the soil in her garden is very loose and crumbly this year as a result of the radishes, with fewer weeds than ever, so I think I'll definitely give the radishes another go before I give up.

Dealing with these radishes and the dry weather we've had so far this spring has really made me ponder something. Am I really a good "vegetable garden" gardener? I love to prune, stake, rearrange, and try new plants in my flower beds. It's harder for me in the vegetable garden.

The garden really annoys me this time of the year because it's so ugly. There's so much bare brown soil, with weeds continually popping up everywhere. The work just seems endless.

Oh, sure, the little sprouts are amazing when they first peek out in the spring. But I've come to the conclusion that I really enjoy the garden best when everything's in full swing—the vegetables are visibly growing, the raised beds are overflowing, plants are blooming, and the whole garden is green. That's when I love going to the garden. I don't even mind the weeds because everything looks so alive and beautiful.

Maybe I just put too much stock in appearances!

MAY

It's the first of May already. Our very warm weather in March made everything a little confusing. Once again I couldn't wait, and I planted the garden too early. Now I sit here twiddling my thumbs, waiting for something to do. The mulching is done already for this spring, also a little early, but we had a family reunion here at our house so I tried to get the spring outside work done earlier than usual.

Last week we had some heavy frosts, and so we gardeners had to cover the tender crops. Some of

Winey's corn plants froze a little bit, and I have some black—meaning frozen—potato plants. I think the potatoes will come back, but I'm not sure about the corn. Lots of strawberries were in full bloom. I'm sure their gardeners made sure to cover those plants in the evening before they went to bed that night.

Last evening I planted cucumbers, summer squash, zinnias, and sunflowers. Every year I plant zinnias and sunflowers in the garden because they're so cheerful and colorful. Zinnias are the toughest flowers I know. They actually like hot, dry weather and thrive in August. They bloom and bloom all summer long, making it possible to bring lovely bouquets of cut flowers into the house.

Meanwhile, I am still waiting for the garden work to really start. Right now there's just a little weeding to do here and there. The first spring onions and radishes are almost ready to pull and eat.

Barbie-Mom's first crop of vegetables isn't quite ready for picking yet.

I know some people have been eating fresh lettuce for a while. I forgot to plant ours earlier. So last week I sprinkled lettuce seeds in my one raised bed, and we'll have some soon. Then I can make "cream lettuce," my favorite spring salad. It's an old-fashioned Amish salad made with spring greens or leaf lettuce, hard-boiled eggs, thinly sliced radishes, and slices of spring onion if you want. You toss everything together and pour a milky, mayonnaise-like dressing over it. Completely yummy! John and the boys don't appreciate it at all, but I can eat an entire bowl by myself.

EARLY MAY

The garden is now completely filled. John helped me plant the remaining corn and potatoes. Then the boys and I set out tiny tomato and pepper plants. They look so fragile with their little woolly stems. I can't imagine how they'll grow, but Winey said that the tomatoes she started by seed and put out when they were tiny, turned out to be her hardiest tomato plants. We'll see what happens to my baby plants.

I went over to Esther's the other night and was just completely inspired to try harder in my garden. Her garden is so lovely! She has small plots of corn and potatoes, other long, narrow, raised beds, and then perfect asparagus and raspberry patches. They all blend together to make a perfect garden. Everything is completely weed-free, and whatever she grows is always so healthy.

Ah, well, maybe someday my garden will be the same. Esther always says that if everything is done—and she means projects around the house—then it's time to move to another house. So I guess I'll be patient about designing and maintaining the perfect garden, because I never want to move away from our house. We built it the year after John and I got married, and already we have so many memories here. I can't imagine what it'll be like when the boys are older. So I'll be satisfied to do things slowly. That way I won't get bored.

The sunflowers are up already, bordering the corn patch. The corn is planted—that's why there are so many weeds. I try to stay out of the garden until the plants are 3-4 inches tall. That way I don't pull out the plants instead of the weeds.

A baby colt's first run in the pasture. She was so tiny when she was born, Winey could pick her up in her arms and carry her.

FRESH TEA

One of our favorite early spring treats from the garden is the first batch of mint tea. We think the earliest tea tastes the best. I'm not sure if it's because we haven't had it for so long, or because those first tender leaves are extra tasty. Regardless of the reason, we are always excited to have the first taste.

It is really quite simple to make and doesn't take long. It's a matter of going to the garden and clipping the tea. I like using the very tip of the stem with just the newest leaves, but some people throw the whole stem of leaves into the boiling water.

Barbie Mom started mixing a few different kinds of mints in one kettle of tea, and the results are wonderful. I was over at her house the other evening, and she was brewing a pot of mint tea that had a handful of lemon balm leaves tossed in. It was absolutely delicious!

MINT TEA

1 quart water

1 large handful mint leaves

Sugar to taste

1. Rinse mint leaves.
2. Bring water to boiling.
3. Remove from heat.
4. Add mint leaves and cover. Let steep for 5 minutes.
5. Remove mint leaves and add sugar to taste, stirring until completely dissolved.
6. Cool before serving.

MAY MENU

Finally we're eating the first spring harvests. Rhubarb has been ready for awhile and also asparagus. I don't have rhubarb in my garden, but Barbie Mom does and always shares it with us.

Sometimes I make a rhubarb sauce, which is thin and a little watery, but delicious over ice cream. Of course, everything that's made with rhubarb needs lots of sugar, so while it's fresh and wonderful, I'm not sure it qualifies as healthy.

RHUBARB SAUCE WITH JELLO

2½ cups chopped rhubarb

⅔ cup sugar

2 cups water

3-oz. box raspberry or strawberry Jello

1. Remove leaves from rhubarb. Wash rhubarb stems thoroughly.
2. Chop rhubarb into small pieces.
3. Stir sugar into water in a stockpot. Bring water and sugar to a boil.
4. Add chopped rhubarb. Cook about 5 minutes, or until soft and slightly stringy.
5. Remove from heat.
6. Stir in Jello.
7. Cool and serve cold. Delicious on pound cake or ice cream!

Rhubarb pie is my absolute favorite, but I've never made one. I'm not a great pie baker, but I'm determined to practice. My boys love pumpkin pie, and John's crazy for shoofly. I'm sure my rating as a cook would get five stars if I'd learn to bake pies.

Aiden and I enjoy asparagus, but everyone else refuses to touch it. Needless to say, I don't have an asparagus patch. Salome has one down on the farm, but her family doesn't eat it either. Still, Barbie Mom always clips some for them and brings us some, too. We usually have it for supper a couple times in the spring, and then that's it. This year I'd like to try an asparagus soup recipe I found. Maybe I can convince the rest of my family to try that.

Fresh radishes and spring onions are always popular. I think most Amish families eat them in the spring. We eat them raw, simply dipped into salt or with dip. My Grandpa Kauffman used to fix a piece of butter bread, layer sliced radishes on top, and sprinkle them with salt. Mom still eats them that way, but I prefer dip. I choose ranch veggie dip, but John likes salt.

My favorite fresh things out of the garden right now are spring greens. Leaf lettuce is growing like wild, and beet leaves are just the right size for cutting and adding to a salad. I love the peppery tang they add to greens.

On Sunday evening we were at Becky's for supper, and she had the best salad I've had in a long time. She cut lettuce and baby beet leaves, pulled some radishes and sliced them thin, and clipped some chive blossoms. We had both read about adding those to dishes, so we wanted to see what they tasted like. They have a mild onion flavor, so we stirred them into the dressing we made for the salad. It looked so beautiful with little lavender, star-shaped flowers resting in the white pool.

After we poured the dressing onto the salad it looked even prettier with the green leaves for a background. We felt very classy with our "gourmet" salad. But it was truly delicious, and everyone agreed that fresh out of the garden can't be beat.

If you let these icicle radishes grow too big, they get really spicy. This size, from Becky's garden, tastes really good.

BEES

Outside work has become much more pleasant since Thomas and Micah wear hats. I know that seems funny, but early this spring they discovered those big, buzzing bumblebees, and they were terrified. Not a little scared and running when they saw them, but truly terrified, stopping in their tracks and screeching bloody murder until someone came to their rescue. That someone, was Mom, of course.

So I'd have to drop what I was doing and go take their hands and lead them to safety. I tried telling them these bees don't sting. John told them that bees are scared of them, but it was Aiden who finally solved the problem. He told his two little brothers that if they wear hats, the bees can't sting them.

The difference was night and day. They'd all clamp their straw hats on their heads and then march outside, not even thinking about bees. They looked so cute because the hats they wore were actually Aiden's old ones—and much too big for Thomas and Micah—but the hats did the trick.

Bees would buzz over their heads, right in front of their noses or all around them, and they didn't blink an eye. They stood there, stalwart little men, waiting until those bees flew away, and then they continued with whatever they were doing.

It was amazing to me, and I always watched with a smile and almost a solemn feeling of awe. I wondered why we grownups can't have that kind of faith? They trusted so completely that Aiden was telling the truth, and they had such faith in their hats. If only we grownups had enough faith to be so completely sure of God's love for us that our bees—our doubts and fears—would never bother us. We'd live our lives secure in his mercy and goodness.

It's been such a lesson to me, and doubly precious because the boys, of course, had no idea about what I've been seeing and thinking. They aren't wearing their hats anymore. They graduated to facing the bees on their own, and they no longer seem to notice them. The hats have served their purpose.

THE BEST TIME OF DAY TO WORK IN THE GARDEN

My favorite time to work in the garden is in the evening. Supper is over, dishes are washed, and the kitchen is closed for the day. The sun is going down behind the barn, and the whole garden and lower lawn lie in shade. Usually the boys are playing on the swing set while I'm happily puttering in the garden.

Even in dry, hot weather there are always weeds to pull and things to check on. It's so important in a garden to keep track of everything, staking or trimming as needed, and just making sure everything's all right. I still like to use my good, old-fashioned hoe and chop up the soil row after row.

It's such a soothing job, hearing the shouts of the boys in the background, birds twittering in the trees, the sun settling behind the mountain after another long day. When I come to the end of the row, I collect the tools and round up my boys. Wearily we traipse into the house for baths and snacks. After tucking three exhausted boys into bed, I settle on the porch for a few minutes of complete silence and solitude before retiring myself.

MAY WEATHER, BEETS, AND PICKLES

This week's weather has been lovely for all growing things, which for a gardener means lots of work. We are ever grateful for the rain, on one hand. But on the other, it also means lots and lots of weeding, especially when it rains almost every day, and then is hot and humid in between. Everything grows like wildfire, weeds and all.

The potatoes shot up at least six inches, and the carrots and cucumbers are healthy. I'm so excited because everything looks fresh and lovely. I know I'll soon be harvesting, canning, and freezing.

First on my list are red beets. I usually pickle them. I only need about five or six quarts because we serve them just for lunch at church. If we

Winey strings bailer twine across her garden for the peas to climb up as they grow.

didn't host church, I probably wouldn't grow beets, because we don't care for them. Well, that's not actually true. Aiden and I love them cooked with a little salt and butter, but the others won't touch them.

Next on my canning agenda are pickles. Pickles are another thing we serve at church, but our family eats them, too. I always make sweet dill pickles. They're almost like regular dill pickles but not as sour. Last year I found a recipe for dill relish, which is quite tasty. I put fresh dill seeds in, and also dried ones, and it is very dilly. It tastes wonderful on hamburgers and hot dogs. I've also stirred it into tuna salad and it adds a lot of zing.

PEAS

Most people are in the midst of pea season. Peas are just ripening, and strawberries will be over soon. I can't believe I'm not doing either. I'll just have to wait until next year for strawberries, and I don't know if I'll ever plant peas again or not. The boys don't like them and neither does John. I serve them in chicken pot pie or soup sometimes, and they eat them in those dishes. But they always need lots of encouragement.

I love fresh peas, but not quite enough to raise them because the picking and the shelling part are so time-consuming . I told my sisters I'd help them with theirs this year. They both have lots of peas in their gardens. You almost have to have help with peas, because one mom with small children has a hard time doing peas by herself. Of course, the boys would like to help, but little boys only help to a certain extent and then, like Mom used to say, "They're more bother than they're worth." For shelling peas, that is!

WINEY'S VISITOR

We all have our own sets of problems in the garden, but I think Winey probably has the most unusual ones right now. She noticed strange footprints in her garden last week. She thought they might be deer prints because they live close to a little woods, and they often see deer around there. But it seemed strange because they were too big for deer, and they were only in the corn.

This was doubly frustrating because Winey planted her corn fairly early, and it was nipped by frost three different times. She thought this was kind of unfair. And now her corn, having been saved from freezing, was being eaten by some varmint!

In the meantime, she realized that Fred, one of her miniature ponies, kept getting out of the pasture whenever he wanted to. He's so small he simply slipped under the bottom strand of wire and wandered wherever he pleased. Winey still didn't get the connection until one night, Fred was in the pasture adjoining the garden. The next morning much more corn was missing, and Winey discovered the culprit! Fred had been slipping under the wire and helping himself at night when he knew no one was around. I think from now on Fred stays inside the *board* fence, and Winey's corn continues to grow!

Shorty and Secret, the tamest of Winey's miniature ponies, behave more like dogs than horses. My boys get them out of their stalls when they visit Winey's house and lead them around. The boys are still a little afraid to ride them.

JUNE

BEETS

Monday turned out to be quite different than I had planned. Monday always means laundry around here and, in the summertime, weeding the garden. I've found out that it works best to have a scheduled day for weeding the garden, because if I do it once a week, it never gets out of control and depressing. Of course there are times when I can't do it precisely every week at exactly the same time, but keeping to that schedule as close as possible is my goal.

This morning it was raining, so I dashed out to the garden and pulled out all the beets. I love to can red beets. It's just too bad we don't enjoy them pickled because they are so easy and fun to preserve. Today I canned seven quarts, and that would probably be plenty, but I have another packet of seeds, so later, towards autumn, I'll plant another crop.

LATE JUNE REFLECTION

Late June is so sad in a way. The first flush of vibrant green is already over for the season, everything's starting to dry out, and it's time to water. The flowers and plants wilt and hang their heads in the hot midday sun.

Green beans are on the menu and also zucchini. My own beans aren't ready because my first planting froze. So I'm waiting. Not really a big loss for our family, as beans are not our favorite vegetable. Last night I saw a few cucumbers hanging on the vines, but there aren't nearly enough to start canning.

Sometimes when I'm working in the garden, I wish it looked like Salome's. Just long, straight rows with no interruptions. Her garden looks so neat and orderly, and mine looks a little scatter-brained this year. I have tomatoes planted in every raised bed, and things stuck in every which way.

I'm seriously considering taking some raised beds out next year so I have a little more space. It's hard for me to believe how fast our family is growing and how much more they're eating all the time. I'm feeling that I hardly have enough space for all the vegetables I want to plant.

Winey's garden is in full bloom with corn and zucchini.
She won't add any additional plants to this garden.

WATERING AND WEEDING

Since it's time to start thinking about watering, I was looking through a stack of old gardening magazines for tips or hints, when I stumbled on a great idea. You rinse out a used plastic milk jug or gallon jug of any kind and prick a few holes in the bottom with a pin. Then you bury the jug halfway into the soil beside a tomato plant and fill it up with water. Slowly the water trickles out, right where the tomato needs it most. I'm excited to try it, and I'm sure Aiden will have fun filling up the empty jugs. He is being quite helpful to me this year, and I think that once he really gets started, he'll quite enjoy his work in the garden.

Last week I was getting ready to mow the lawn, and I noticed that the corn needed weeding. So I got the boys started with that while I mowed, and I was completely shocked. They did a wonderful job. They pulled every weed and put them into their bucket. And then Aiden even emptied the bucket and stowed it carefully in the toolshed.

I was so proud of them and thanked them profusely, to which Thomas drily remarked, "Well, it was just me and Aiden. Micah didn't do one single thing!" (Thomas is three; Micah is two!)

JULY

The first of July can be so depressing in the garden. Everything needs water badly. The flowers and lawn are brown and sad, and the garden is fast becoming a dry, tangled mess.

The corn is not thriving at all. And for some reason, the cucumbers have a blight and I'm afraid I won't get any at all. The zucchini is wilting and I'm trying to keep the bugs away. But it seems that once they get started on a plant, it's hard to get rid of them.

Always at this time of the year I want to throw my hands in the air and just give up. The weather has been unrelenting. We've had weeks of hot, dry days with no rain in sight. The tomatoes look nice and I'm thankful for that. I need lots of those. But everything else is a real struggle.

RAIN

A little rain makes such a huge difference! Yesterday we had a few good showers, and it's unbelievable how refreshed everything looks. I did the laundry this morning and then walked down to the garden to check for weeds and to see if there's anything I should be doing.

I was pleasantly surprised with everything. The corn that I was so worried about is doing really well. I think with all the watering, we might have a nice crop. I'm sure I'll still have to buy corn this year. The boys love corn, and chicken corn soup is a favorite of ours. So I need lots of corn.

If I have to buy corn or any other vegetables, I usually call our family friend who goes to the local produce auction every Tuesday in the summer. He's an excellent auction shopper because he has the patience to wait until the end, when the prices aren't as high anymore. He's gotten great buys on corn for almost everyone in my family. All we have to do is call him, and he delivers the vegetables to our door.

My tomatoes look wonderful. I really think the plastic-gallon-jug watering system may be the reason. It works well, and it's so little work for the gardener, that I'm extolling its virtue every-where I go. I think Winey is going to try it, and I'm using all the jugs I can get. I don't have a lot because we stopped buying milk at the grocery store.

We buy our milk from Elvin and Salome down on the farm, but this summer I've been buying two percent milk for myself, because the milk from the farm seems so rich and fattening. In the summer we drink lots of iced coffee in the evening, and I feel too guilty to enjoy the coffee when I make it with that fattening milk. So the milk jugs are going to good use as watering sys-tems.

I'm still holding out hope for the cucumbers. This morning I thought they looked a bit perkier, so they may snap out of it. I'm just really envious. Everyone else is canning pickles already, and I'm still hoping my plants survive.

Ah, well, that's the story of a gardener's life. I wonder if anyone who has a garden always gets the produce they want every year. I'm just thank-ful that the tomatoes are compensating for my cucumbers.

My sunflowers, some more than 12-feet tall, are at their prettiest now.

WATERING

Now we have a new ritual in the evening. After the supper dishes are washed and put away, I make sure the porches are swept for the day. Then I go down to the garden for evening watering. The best time to water is late evening or early morning. I like to water at the end of the day because the plants can soak it up all night before the sun gets too hot.

John set up our drip-line for the corn this week, and the difference is amazing. The drip-line is a series of plastic pipes running the length of the rows. Each pipe has little evenly spaced holes all along its length. The pipes are all joined together, with a hose fastened on the one end. When the water is turned on, it rushes into all the pipes, and water drips right at the base of the plants. So there's very little evaporation.

Just a few days of watering and the corn looks brand-new. I wish water would make such a difference for the cucumbers. They look pathetic. John said they may recover, so I guess we'll wait and see.

Winey has canned 20 quarts of pickles already and her plants are still going strong, so maybe I can get some from her. That's the lovely part of living in a close-knit community like ours. If people have something extra in their gardens, they put the word out, and anyone is welcome to the extras. Last year my cucumbers didn't do very well either, and Aunt Eva gave me all her extras, so we had plenty of pickles this past winter.

Since we serve pickles for church lunch, I always need plenty of them. We eat some but not a whole lot. The boys go through stages. For a while they won't eat any at all, and the next time I serve them, they'll eat half a quart. So I never really know how the mood will strike them.

The other thing I like to do with cucumbers is make relish. The dill relish I discovered last year calls for cucumbers. It's absolutely delicious and it really adds zing to any sandwich, especially burgers done on the grill.

Esther just planted corn in this portion of her garden after an earlier crop ended. John's grandmother says that you can plant corn until the 4th of July, but I think that's taking a chance because it might not have time to ripen.

DILL CUCUMBER RELISH

8 lbs. cucumbers

½ cup salt

2 tsp. ground turmeric

4 cups water

2½ cups finely
   chopped onions

⅓ cup sugar

2 Tbsp. dill seeds

4 cups white wine vinegar

1. Using a food processor or grinder, finely chop cucumbers.
2. Place cucumbers in a glass or stainless steel bowl.
3. Sprinkle with salt and turmeric.
4. Pour water over cucumbers and spices. Stir. Let stand for 2 hours.
5. Drain cucumbers thoroughly. Rinse with clean water and press down, removing extra liquid.
6. Pour drained cucumbers into large saucepan, and add remaining ingredients.
7. Bring to a boil over medium high heat.
8. Boil gently, stirring occasionally, about 10 minutes, or until vegetables are heated through.
9. Ladle relish into jars, add lids, and process according to your canner's instructions.

This summer we eat outside on the back porch almost every evening. After you start that, it seems stifling to eat inside. Then I do dishes and water the garden while John does his evening chores. We take our baths and sit on the front porch to watch the sun sink behind the mountains.

We are porch-sitters in the summertime. It's a little cooler outside in the evening. Our house stays fairly cool, but always by late afternoon, it's quite warm inside. So we tend to stay outside on the porches until bedtime. Usually by then it feels better inside, especially when we start the fans running.

Hauling a full bucket of cucumbers
and tomatoes out of Winey's garden.

A SURPRISE JULY RAIN

"What is so rare as a day in June?" The line should be, "What is so rare as a rainy weekend in July?" We were blessed this weekend with rain and drizzly clouds for two days. What a godsend for the gardens, lawns, hayfields, and everything in between. Watering is fine and works well for a garden, but there's nothing as great as good old rain. Everything is magically green again!

Today I have to mow the grass after weeks of not doing anything in the lawn. The garden, too, is crying out for attention. Weeds pop out overnight

after a rain. The forecast for today is sunny with a chance of thunderstorms this afternoon. So as soon as everything dries off a bit, I'll head outside. What fun! My favorite kind of day.

Later this week I'll probably freeze some corn. Amazingly, our corn is turning out to be very nice. Last week Winey and I did 54 dozen ears of corn that a friend of ours got (for a wonderful price, I might add) at the local produce auction.

Doing corn is such a mess, so we try to work outside as much as possible. Winey has a nice back porch, so we set up tables there, and large plastic tubs, where we cooled the corn after cooking it inside on her stove. We cut it off the cobs outdoors, too, and bagged it.

We were very pleased after we were all done. What a feeling of accomplishment to take all our corn to the freezer and stack it neatly in preparation for this winter.

We keep a chest freezer in the neighbor's garage, and then pay them yearly for the electricity it uses. Sometimes it's quite a pain to have to scooter down the hill to stock up on frozen foods, but Mom says it's better this way. They used to have their food in cold storage in a town miles away, so they got their frozen food only when they went to town.

It's time to gear up for more canning and freezing. Peaches are ready now, and the tomatoes are ripening more every day. Making applesauce is a major project for me, but that will come a little later.

Everyone else is done with their green beans, but I'm still patiently waiting for mine, which are blooming now. I just hope I can do them before we go to the beach during the first week in August. I'm trying to get a lot of preserving done before we go, so that when we return, I won't be completely overwhelmed.

Tomatoes will be in full swing then. I'm hoping I won't have to buy tomatoes, but mine are looking a little blighty.

AUGUST

August is definitely the busy season for gardeners. Our garden looks scrappy, and weeds are hiding everywhere. And I'm up to my elbows in canning and freezing.

I went out to the garden to pick the first batch of corn, all ready to freeze some, and wow, I had a big surprise! The ears were very thin with parched kernels. There wasn't enough corn to freeze, and hardly even enough for one meal. But I told John that was the early corn which we hadn't watered soon enough, and there's nothing that ruins corn like not enough water.

The second batch has looked much better, and I've been very excited about it. But we had a thunderstorm the other evening with heavy rain and flattening wind. The next morning when I looked

out at the garden, our beautiful corn patch was almost flat. John's mom told me it will straighten out a little bit and the corn will still ripen. It will just be hard to pull it off the stalks. I am so disappointed!

Some of the gigantic sunflowers blew over, too, and that surprised me because they are really sturdy. Sunflowers have a great root system, and they can usually withstand a lot of wind. They're hard to pull out in the fall, but I guess this wind was extra strong.

Aiden and I went to pull the damaged ones out the whole way, and we were shocked at how tall they were. Some were at least 12 feet tall. And of course, typical me, I didn't write down what kind they were, so if I want to plant that particular variety again, I'll have to guess.

Aiden thought the stems would work perfectly to make a log cabin like Pa Ingalls did in *Little House on the Prairie*. So he spent the afternoon clipping off the flower heads to save for the birds, sawing off the root ends, and trimming the leaves. It was so cute how hard he worked on his little project, and now he has a little stack of sunflower stems waiting to be made into a cabin.

I didn't have the heart to tell him that he'll need many, many more before he's ready to build, because he was so enthused. Knowing him, he'll start building, and everything won't be exactly like he imagined, and then he'll be so disappointed he'll just stop. He's such a little perfectionist. If something's not quite up to par, he gets so frustrated that he quits. I'm afraid he'll have to learn a few lessons about that when he gets to school.

GARDEN INVADERS

Another huge disappointment. After I came back from a week at the beach with my family, I discovered that all our gorgeous corn had been completely demolished by an animal. We're almost certain it was a raccoon, although it could have been a skunk.

Because the thunderstorm had caused the corn to fall over, it was conveniently placed for creatures, and they surely made good use of it. There was still enough left that I could pick corn for suppers, and then it was gone.

At least I had done most of my corn already, but I wanted this batch of corn for soup. I like to have whole-grain corn for soup, so I cut it off the cob with a knife and freeze it like that instead of creaming it. I guess we'll have chicken corn soup made with creamed corn this year. And that works. I made it like that all last winter. But I wanted to have some cut corn this year.

TOMATOES

I'm getting a little concerned about the tomato crop. I wanted a lot of tomatoes, and it doesn't look very promising. Once again, the plants themselves are huge, but I really have to look for the fruit. The tomatoes that are there seem pretty small.

I'm having a real problem with the ends of the tomatoes turning black. Becky told me the plants need calcium. Winey sprinkles dry milk around hers and waters it down, so I guess I'll have to try that. Crushing up Tums and sprinkling those around the plants is supposed to help, too. I did that, but it takes an awful lot of Tums for all my tomatoes.

I'm really concentrating on watering the tomatoes now. John's mom says you can hardly water them too much. My milk jug project is still underway, but I discovered that the plants need regular watering by hose, too.

This week I canned my first batch of pizza sauce, and it turned out really well. The tomatoes were small, and it took quite a bit for one batch

of sauce, but, my, it was tasty! Thomas and Micah were even smacking their lips when they tried it. One by one the boys would come in the door, sniff, and say, "M-m-m what do I smell?"

Aiden thought he smelled garlic bread, and Thomas declared he smelled stromboli. So I guess they were both partly right since pizza sauce smells like oregano and garlic.

CANNING

One by one I'm checking off my August projects. Number one was pickles. Yes, August is a little late to be canning pickles, but my own amounted to almost nothing. So I had to wait until someone gave me their leftovers. Winey let me pick from her plants, and I got lots of nice cucumbers. I tried Becky's recipe using dill seeds and some fresh dill heads, which look very nice. I'm hoping they'll taste good. They looked beautiful when I took them out of the canner.

I also did peaches, which is not my favorite job. But the boys like them so well that I always do plenty. Last year I tried something new and canned our peaches with a glaze. They were very tasty, but they tended to get brown and discolored over time. We could still eat them, but discoloration seemed to affect the flavor, and they just weren't quite as good. So this year I've canned them plain with water and sugar. They look nice, and I'm sure we'll enjoy them all winter.

I enjoy it when the boys help me in the kitchen. But there comes a time when you have to say, "Okay, go outside now." I think they like to spend time in the kitchen when I'm canning because I need tools I rarely use and do things that I don't normally do.

It's such a good feeling to spend a day preserving food, then carefully wipe off the jars, and take them down to the basement the next morning. My canning shelves are starting to have the mid-summer look—freshly canned pickles, peaches, relishes, and red beets. The tomato products shelf still looks a little bare, as does the applesauce, but we're still in August. Those things still need to be done.

Does anyone beside the Amish use Victorio Strainers? It's what I've always used to make applesauce. First, I cut the apples in quarters (I cut out any bruises or soft spots, but I don't remove the stem or the core, though many people do.). Then I cook the apples until they're soft enough to put through the strainer. We pour the cooked apples into the top of the strainer and then we turn the handle, forcing the seeds and skin out through a side funnel. The strained applesauce runs down the white tray into the bucket.

We probably eat more applesauce than anything else at our house. Every time we eat pizza we have to eat applesauce, too. And John eats lots of applesauce in his soup. He has a very specific routine. First he crumbles saltines in his soup. Next, he pours applesauce into his bowl on top of the soup, and then he eats his soup and applesauce together.

SALSA

The last official canning project of summer is done. Becky spent the day here at my house, and we did four batches of salsa.

Salsa is one thing I used to never insist on having home-canned. I thought I could buy some that tasted just as good. Ah, I was greatly mistaken!

Salsa done right, made with Becky's recipe, is absolutely unbeatable. It turned out so well, and we had so much fun making it, that it ended the whole canning season on a happy note.

SEPTEMBER

APPROACHING AUTUMN

Welcome September! A month of gorgeous days and cool nights. The bulk of garden work is done for the season, and everything looks almost ready for winter.

I thought I had wrapped up canning for the year, but then I couldn't resist doing a bit more!

This week I did more pizza sauce and finished canning applesauce. I still have some tomatoes in the garden, but the plants themselves are dying fast.

I was so surprised this week when I did a bushel of tomatoes that a friend brought me. He got them at an auction, and I was so pleased with the beautiful Roma tomatoes. I thought surely these will make gorgeous sauce. They were huge and firm and bright red. But I was shocked at how the sauce turned out.

I soon discovered that the tomatoes were so watery that I had to drain them fully or the puree would have been as thin as tomato juice. The pizza sauce that I made with my own small Roma tomatoes turned out much better. It's a lot thicker and has more of a tomato taste.

I guess that's just the difference between tomatoes grown a little on the dry side or tomatoes grown with plenty of water. I'm so glad for Barbie Mom's advice about giving tomatoes lots of water. I certainly saw the contrast this year.

SUNFLOWERS

What a happy surprise the sunflowers were in the long run! This summer they were gorgeous, like tall sentinels keeping watch over the garden. Then when their flowers turned heavy and drooping, they looked a little sad.

After two or three heavy thunderstorms they appeared completely lost, and some of them were even uprooted. That's when the work really began, and I started to regret every single seed I had dropped in the ground. They're huge and tough to uproot and drag away. But we succeeded, with John's help, of course, and slowly but surely cleared the garden of all sunflowers.

I saved about three-fourths of the flower heads and carefully stored them on a make-shift table in the hayloft. They've dried nicely. This fall, when I began to feed the birds wholeheartedly, I decided to try the sunflower seeds.

At first I thought we'd have to loosen the seeds and put them into a bird feeder. So Aiden and I spent quite some time filling the feeders. All of a sudden, I thought, "Why not just fasten a whole flower head to the bird feeder and let the birds pick out the seeds themselves?" So that is what we did, and it works perfectly.

I've noticed that nuthatches and woodpeckers tend to like them more than the other birds. Sometimes I have to change them before the seeds are all gone, if the weather's been wet and rainy, because they tend to get a little soggy. But I've been so pleased with the whole endeavor. I'll definitely do it again next year. The seed heads look so charming tucked in the suet holders on the bird feeder or simply tied in a tree with a piece of baler twine. It looks so simple and homey.

This year I'm really stepping up my bird-feeding. Twice this fall we've seen pileated woodpeckers in our little woods beyond the house. I don't know if I could lure them into the yard or not, but I'm sure going to try all winter long.

I love feeding birds. There's something so charming about birds at a feeder. I'm always struck by their pecking order. The bigger birds always get first choice. If a woodpecker or a cardinal happens to be at the feeder at the same time, there may be quite a racket until they decide whose turn it is.

If only they would all be like the little juncos, who eat leftovers off the ground and never make a fuss about anything. They're such pretty birds with their gray backs and white undersides. They look as if they've been dipped in milk.

The boys liked how big the pumpkins grew this year. But they were still too small to eat, so I was disappointed. We did carve one Jack-o-Lantern, and we decorated the porch with them. I will try neck pumpkins next year and make a pumpkin pie for my boys.

CLEAN UP

Everybody is starting to clear out their gardens now. Winey's is completely empty, but she did hers early because they have church at their house this weekend. Becky said her garden is covered in weeds, but I didn't notice when I was there. Her zinnias still look beautiful.

Last night I walked up to Esther's to buy some eggs. Her garden's still looking good. She has some corn coming yet and radishes again, and her pumpkins are almost ripe. I wish I'd be more like her. She never seems to get tired of gardening.

I really enjoy our garden, but always, always, toward the end of August I'm sick of it. I just want to tear everything out, get rid of all the weeds, and take a break for awhile.

This fall I'm going to attempt tillage radishes again. Everyone thinks I'm crazy since I didn't have a great turnout last time, but I didn't do those right. This week we want to pull out the corn and then plant radishes.

Hopefully it will rain soon after that, and they'll pop up right away. Then they'll grow tall before the first frost comes, and everything will go according to plan. The seeds will sprout, the plants will grow big, freeze, die out, and enrich the soil over winter. In the spring we'll till them into the soil, and they'll do wonders for our garden.

RADISHES

Absolutely unbelievable! In one week, all the tillage radishes are sprouting and the garden is turning green. I looked out the window this morning, and I thought, "Is that not radishes already?" Sure enough, I believe every seed sprouted. I am amazed at how fast they popped up, but we did have the perfect weather. It rained for four days and was really warm—ideal "sprouting" weather.

The tomatoes have started growing again, but I'm done gardening for this year. The squash bugs got my pattypans, and that was all right with me. No one was in the mood for squash anymore. The peppers are still going strong, but I've used the last ones I want for salsa. I think peppers never stop producing until frost. The banana peppers were terrific this year. The zinnias and marigolds are still pretty, but the remaining sunflowers are

drooping badly.

Last week there was an article in our local newspaper about planting a fall garden, including lettuce, radishes to eat, onions, and early spring crops. I almost fell for it, imagining that fresh, crunchy lettuce and radish salad. But when I thought hard about it, I realized that I don't want to be gardening on into the autumn.

We have church at our house this fall, and I'll try to have the garden cleared out by then. It looks so much neater, and it also means that when church is over, I can relax and start some wintertime projects, instead of dragging out the gardening season.

Having church is always rather nerve-wracking, because you spend weeks beforehand cleaning everything inside and out. It is a good time to get some projects done that you might not do as often, if it weren't for church.

WINDING DOWN

The garden continues to slowly wind down for the season. The squash and cucumbers are among the first to go. They turn brown and ugly, and the only thing to do is just pull them up and throw them away. We have a throw-away pile at the edge of the weeds, so I always use a wheelbarrow and cart everything there as I clean up.

I'm still trying to decide whether pole beans or regular green beans work better in my garden. The pole beans, which produce green beans, looked very pretty growing up an old wooden stepladder I found. I liked that they grew up instead of spreading out. But I didn't care for the fact that, whenever it got too windy, and we get lots of wind here,

the plants and the whole ladder support would weave back and forth.

Finally, during the one storm we had, the wind toppled the whole ladder and pulled the beans' roots right out of the ground. That was the end of the pole beans. Luckily, I had planted regular green beans, too, and those are the ones I froze.

Our beans were late, and now the time is here to clean out that bed, too. The corn is finished, and we've dug the potatoes. I'd still enjoy a few fresh tomatoes yet, but the plants are really turning brown in the middle. It's only a matter of time until they're gone.

Autumn is closer than we think. Everywhere there are signs small and large.

The biggest change for our family is the start of school. This is our first year as school parents, and what changes that will bring to all of us!

Every morning now, the boys have to get up at seven o'clock so we're all ready to head out the door at five 'til eight. Thomas, Micah, and I walk out the driveway, while Aiden pushes his scooter alongside. We wait at the end of the drive until Salome's children arrive, then Aiden joins the group and they're off. They scooter almost two miles to school, and how Aiden enjoys it!

Thomas and Micah have adjusted quickly to playing by themselves, and I find I have more time to myself for some reason! This week I should be finishing up in the garden. There are still raised beds to clear out, but I've been busy in the house. It's time to start the annual fall housecleaning.

Most people do their main housecleaning in the spring, but we have an outdoor furnace, so our house really doesn't get that dirty in the winter. I prefer doing housecleaning in the fall, because I think the house gets dirtier in the summer with everyone in and out all day long. Plus our windows and doors are open all the time, which makes for lots of dusty corners.

Last week I finished the upstairs, so I'll work on the main floor this week. Housecleaning is so much hard work, but I actually enjoy it once I'm started and in the middle of it.

Mariah, Becky's wheezing bulldog, keeps watch over the canning jars.

Aiden usually takes a turkey sandwich to school, along with a cookie or brownie, grapes,
and something salty in the red cooler that rides in his scooter basket.

OCTOBER

Finally this week I finished cleaning out the garden. Everything is gone for the year except the carrots. My sister-in-law told me that carrots stay good all autumn and into the winter if you pile hay on top of them in the fall. It keeps

them from freezing for quite a while. I think I'll try it since Thomas and Micah absolutely adore carrots.

While I was cleaning out the garden this week, they spent all day eating carrots. They would each pull one out, run up to the barn to rinse it at the hydrant, then come back to the garden and sit on the edge of the raised beds to enjoy their snack. When we went inside for lunch, the garden was strewn with carrot tops and the boys' mouths had suspicious brown rings around them. As the morning wore on, the carrots that were being eaten were a little less clean! Ah, well. I guess eating dirt hasn't harmed them so far. I'm not sure why they enjoy fruits and vegetables more when they can pick them, even though they're full of dirt when they find them.

Salome cleaned out her garden and tilled the soil so she could plant tillage radishes like I did this year.

BEAUTIFUL OCTOBER WEATHER!

My favorite time of year is definitely autumn. I love the crisp air and the leaves swirling to the ground. Fall does mean the end of gardening season, but everything else is so lovely. The tall grasses planted right by the garden are perfect in October. They're all in bloom, and their huge feathery plumes wave in the wind. The slight-est little breeze sets them asway, and they are gorgeous.

TILLAGE RADISHES

The garden looks so beautiful because the tillage radishes are a lush green field. The raised beds are bare, waiting for their covering of compost. The sunflowers have all been taken down and dragged to the burn pile. Aiden abandoned his idea of a log cabin, and the sunflower stalks are all in a pile by the trash, slowly wilting, turning crispy and brown, waiting to be burned.

CHURCH AT OUR HOUSE

Having church means lots of work, including cleaning everything thoroughly inside and out. We have church services in our basement because that's the room with the most space. But not only the basement needs to be cleaned. The whole house must be clean upstairs and down.

There are people all through the house the day of church, because women with babies usually put their babies down for naps upstairs. That means making what we call "floor nests" (blankets on the floor) for naps.

When people first arrive, the women and girls congregate on the first floor, usually in the kitchen and living room area, while the men and boys gather in the barn. Yes, the barn needs to be clean and organized, as well.

When it's time for the services to start, everyone files into the basement where benches and chairs have been arranged in straight rows. The men and boys sit on one side of the room, facing the women and girls on the other side. The ministers sit in the middle, making a kind of

dividing line, I guess. Church services last for three hours.

When church is over, the benches are turned into two long tables, one set on each side of the basement. In short order, the benches are covered with tablecloths and dishes, and lunch is served.

We always serve the same thing for lunch, with small variations. This year I had pumpkin pies because Salome had lots of pumpkins in her garden and offered to bake the pies for me.

Church women always bring bread. So we have sliced bread with a peanut butter spread and a cheese spread, plus butter and jelly. Served alongside the bread and different spreads, we have pickles and pickled red beets. Most people add sliced deli meat like ham or bologna and often seasoned pretzels. They're regular small pretzels that are covered with a dry powdery seasoning used for making ranch-flavored dip. They're yummy dipped in cheese spread. There's coffee and water to drink, and that rounds out the meal.

Men and boys eat at one table and women and girls at the other one. When the first group is done eating, the dirty dishes are quickly washed, the food replenished, and a second group is seated and fed. Usually the tables are filled two times, with one table being set once more for anyone who didn't get to eat before. After everyone has had lunch, people start to leave and church is officially over.

NOVEMBER

A TIME TO RELAX AND REFLECT

Every morning now, the grass is silver with ice. Slowly the leaves are disappearing from the trees, and flower beds are turning into barren landscapes of dirt and twigs. It's a melancholy time of year for gardeners. Everything's finished for this year, and it's a little early to plan for next year.

The summer just past already seems far away. I can hardly remember the joys of my garden. I think every gardener needs this time of not thinking about the garden to really be ready for the next year. Our garden is completely ugly and bare, except for the radishes. They still look lush and green.

THANKSGIVING

We hosted Thanksgiving dinner for my family this year. After lunch my brother took a stroll around the garden and came into the house with a handful of radishes. "Why in the world wouldn't you eat these, Laura? You have a whole field of them!"

I told him radishes aren't my favorite unless I have them in salad, and besides, I didn't think these tillage radishes were good to eat.

Well, he proceeded to wash them in my kitchen sink and asked for a cutting board. In short order he had them washed, sliced, and sprinkled with salt. They actually weren't bad! They tasted like a mixture of

mild radishes and turnips. Okay, I guess they're good if that's the kind of thing you like.

John ate a couple of them after my brother was gone, but he soon got tired of them. So now we have a crop of radishes just waiting to freeze in the ground. We did have deer in the garden, and I think they're enjoying the radish tops. That's all right as long as they stay out of our garden crops in the summer.

DECEMBER

DECEMBER EVENINGS

Ah, the difference in our evenings now! Around four-thirty or five o'clock, I have to turn the gas light on. We thought we might use battery lights this winter, but I don't really like them for long, cold evenings. Gas light is so much cozier. I make supper by lamplight, and we eat long after dark. Of course I'm washing dishes by lamplight, too.

Sometimes it's hard to be patient with the boys during these long evenings, because they really are bursting with energy after supper. They can't just run out the door now and spend the evening outside, like they do when it's warm. Legos and books keep them entertained for only so long, and then they have to move.

I've finally agreed to let them play their version of hockey in the house. They hit a small plastic ball back and forth on the family-room floor, with many shouts, cheers, and exclamations of "goalie!"

I thought it was absolutely too noisy, but I forced myself to accept the fact that boys don't play quiet games. Or if they do, they don't stay with them for long at all. So now they happily play noisy games until bath-time, and then it's time to pick up toys and do something quiet until bedtime.

RADISHES CONTINUE WITH US

Gardening season is really over now. The tillage radishes were green and healthy all autumn, and now they're starting to turn brown and fall over.

There's one thing that's so surprising to me, and I never imagined it before. Radishes have a horrible scent as they're decomposing.

The other day I walked outside and thought I smelled something. I couldn't quite decide what it was and finally chalked it up as manure. Since we live with farms all around us, I just assumed someone was hauling manure, until John came in the other evening and asked if I was down by the garden lately. No, I said I hadn't been. He wondered if I smelled anything strange lately, and I told him I had, and that I couldn't figure out what it was.

Imagine my surprise when he said it comes from the garden. The radishes are starting to break down and decompose, and they definitely have the unmistakable scent of decaying vegetables. Good for next year's garden!

We have a holiday the day after Christmas called Second Christmas, and we were with my family that day. And so soon it's all over until next year. I always ask myself, "Am I truly grateful for all the gifts God gives me throughout the year?" There's so much to be thankful for, not only over the holidays but every day.

This year I baked many cookies for different Christmas get-togethers. The boys love to help, especially with cut-out cookies. Usually I let them help me, but sometimes I find my patience wearing thin. After we clean up our cookie-baking mess, we go outside for a while.

PLAIN TO BEAUTIFUL

I always have a few antique trunks to refinish in the wintertime, since people know I prefer to do them when I don't have outside work. Refinishing trunks is a little project I started before I got married, and I still enjoy doing it. It's time-consuming, slow, careful work, but I find it so satisfying to see how truly beautiful something so old and ragged can become. I guess it's sort of like gardening in a way—turning something plain into a thing of beauty.

ABOUT THE AUTHOR

Laura Anne Lapp, a member of the Amish church, lives with her husband and three sons in a tucked-away valley in central Pennsylvania. Before her marriage, she was a teacher in an Amish school for eight years. Gardening is the highlight of her year.

ABOUT THE PHOTOGRAPHER

Jeremy Hess heads the team of Jeremy Hess Photographers, based in Lancaster, Pennsylvania.